LIBRARY

In
Memory
of
Fannie
B.
Klinkenberg

Klinkenberg Memorial Fund

FARM TOWN

FARM TOWN

A MEMOIR OF THE 1930'S

PHOTOGRAPHS BY J. W. McMANIGAL

EDITED, WITH TEXT AND ADDITIONAL

PHOTOGRAPHS, BY GRANT HEILMAN

The Stephen Greene Press · Brattleboro · Vermont · 1974

Copyright © 1974 by Grant Heilman.

This book has been produced in the United States of America. It is designed by R. L. Dothard Associates, composed by American Book–Stratford Press, Inc., printed by Nimrod Press, bound by Robert Burlen & Son, Inc., and published by The Stephen Greene Press.

McManigal, J. W.
    Farm town: a memoir of the 1930's.

    1. Farm life—Middle West—Pictorial works.
I. Heilman, Grant, 1919– II. Title.
S521.5.M53M3 917.7′03′3 73–86031
ISBN 0–8289–0205–4
ISBN 0–8289–0204–6 (pbk.)

74 75 76 77 78 79 9 8 7 6 5 4 3 2 1

Contents

BACK THEN . . .   6

SPRING   9

HAYING   19

THRESHING   23

CORN PICKING   35

DOWNTOWN   43

THE SALE   53

THE FAIR   57

POLITICS   63

CHORES   67

LEISURE   75

WINTER   79

WHATEVER HAPPENED TO HORTON?   87

A TECHNICAL NOTE   96

Back then...

THE PHOTOGRAPHS in this book were taken by J. W. McManigal, almost entirely in and around his home town of Horton, Kansas, between 1935 and 1940. The farming there was typical of farming almost everywhere in the United States at the time, for it was largely before the days of specialization.

The barnyard flock of hens, the handful of cows and the hand-turned separator, the pigs butchered in the back yard—they're all here in the book, but have since disappeared from reality. That farming was essentially subsistence farming, with some left over for the market. Now it's market farming, with minimal interest in self-sufficiency, except as it helps the household budget. Ask a young farmer whether he can butcher a hog, or ask his wife to show you her homemade bread: you'll see a lot of uncomprehending stares.

Wes McManigal was born in Horton in 1892, and by the time he was sixteen he was supporting his family as a linotype operator. After World War I, when he was severely wounded and was captured by the Germans, he went through a series of American hospitals before he was able to return to Horton.

He worked on the local weekly paper as business manager until one afternoon in 1934, when he simply walked out. He was fed up with his job. Almost overnight he became a professional photographer. Although he always claimed he would rather photograph pretty girls, there was more demand for pictures of farming, and he quickly established himself as an agricultural photographer. His wife, Tag, ran the office, and Wes roamed the surrounding countryside picturing his friends at work. Eventually his passion for photography cooled, and he became Postmaster in Horton, with his photography business continuing as a sideline.

Wes and I had become friends through a book he had written for Tom Maloney of *U.S. Camera Magazine*—a down-to-earth, common-sense book called *Marketing Your Pictures—How and Where*. The book had been published just as I was beginning my own career. As a

6

result, for a number of years Wes acted as an agent for the sales of my pictures along with his own.

By 1963 he had retired from photography, and I began to be haunted by the thought of his file of negatives sitting in his damp, unheated office. I didn't know what I would do with them, but I offered to buy them. I drove to Horton, spent two days combing through his files, bought the entire eight thousand negatives, and brought them back home. It was then, seeing them all together, I realized what a beautiful record of rural life they were.

Wes died in 1970, but Tag, his widow, was living in Horton, and so were many of his favorite subjects—and friends. I thought a book should be made of his work, so I went to Horton equipped with a set of prints of his most interesting pictures.

Tag McManigal is one of those remarkable small-town people who knows everyone, and with her as my guide we sat in farm kitchens, in shady yards under Chinese elms, and even in a cooler full of sides of beef, and talked with people whom Wes had photographed. We showed them both the pictures they were in, and others we thought they would recall. We wandered through barns, along dusty roads, and into the backs of country stores.

I've done a good many interviews for various purposes, but never have any been so much fun. The hours slipped by and the notes became more extensive and I couldn't have worked with more pleasant people. So, unless otherwise indicated, all the quotations with the pictures in this book are from people I interviewed around Horton.

It became evident that many readers would ask: "But whatever happened to Horton?" After all, Wes McManigal covered only a tiny slice of time. Therefore while I interviewed I also did a number of "after" pictures to match Wes's "before" photographs. But it's really his book—his and Tag's and the people he pictured.

Lititz, Pennsylvania, October 1973   GRANT HEILMAN

WES MCMANIGAL

SPRING

ON THE FARM, spring's a time of coming alive. I talked to an old farmer once about spring tonics, and he said: "You don't need a spring tonic. Spring *is* a tonic."

It's hard to explain the joy of walking a rough furrow behind a team of sweaty horses, or of worrying whether your rows of green seedling corn will show up evenly. But the joy was there, and the pride of accomplishing a tiring chore was real.

The field work in Kansas was slightly different from that in many other sections of the country, for they used a lister—a lister plow—to prepare their fields for planting. Essentially, a lister is a double moldboard plow which throws the ground into furrows and ridges; seeds are dropped onto the ridges. A common cultivating tool used then was also different from most other places: it was called a "sled curler," and it piled soil around corn plants when they were only about three inches high. It weeded the soil, gave more protection to the young plants, and heightened the ridges.

Otherwise, farming technique in Kansas was much like that in most other sections of the country.

My dad used to sow clover by hand. He used only his thumb and first finger to spread the clover and it always came up wonderfully even.

When we plowed in hot weather we'd often have two teams and switch at the end of the field to let one rest while we used the other one. But the driver, he just kept going.

He was so proud of that tractor. It's all dolled up with a
light, and look at his *Flying Red Horse* up there on the
hood. That tractor must have been made about 1938 or
1939. We still have one just the same age, but with rubber
tires. With a three-bottom plow, it cost a thousand and
fifty dollars new. I can remember the price exactly.

That's a fine set of work harness, must have cost a hundred dollars when they bought it. And look at the little pretty down there, shaped like a heart. The neck yoke isn't much though.

That's got to be two separate rigs: six horses on the lister, and the two closest are planting. With listing we usually put four or six abreast.

By the time I was nine I was running a New Departure cultivator. We had to do ten acres a day to put in a good day's work. If you figure it out with forty-inch corn rows, a quarter-mile long, it took ten rows to make an acre, and that was two and a half miles of walking. So in a day we had to walk twenty-five miles in the furrow. Course we milked the cows in the morning before we went to the fields, and milked again in the evening when we got home—then we had supper.

But Wes McManigal's pictures show cultivating from a seat. That was a damn sight easier than walking the furrow.

HAYING

IT'S THE EARLIEST of the harvests. In the 1930's hay was usually cut with a mower, raked by hand into piles, then forked by hand onto wagons, and finally lifted, frequently with horse power, into the barn mow.

By the late Thirties, balers were beginning to be seen. At first they were so bulky they were stationary, and anything to be baled was brought in to the baler. But gradually they were made more compact and could be towed through the fields attached to a tractor. Early balers required as many as five men to operate them— a baler is a complicated machine which will pick up hay from the field, compress it into a box shape, then twist wire, or tie twine, around the bale.

Nowadays, farmers go off to the hayfield alone with a baler behind their tractor, a bale thrower on the end of the baler, and a wagon behind that. The only extra manpower needed is on the spare wagons to run the baled hay to storage places.

But even this is changing. There is chopped hay and haylage, which can be moved around by being blown through tubes by air pressure. And now there are giant stacking machines that pick up the hay, compress it, and form it into six- or eight-ton stacks which are handled completely mechanically. The changes almost always represent greater capital investment, less labor, and increased speed: and that's the direction agriculture has always gone.

19

My daughter loves horses but she never had to ride a horse back and forth all day, lifting hay up into the barn. After while it got pretty boring.

We would thresh stacked wheat all through the fall back then. It took a lot of know-how to make the stacks right, so they'd repel rain.

THRESHING

NOTHING was quite so romantic as grain harvesting—nor such hot work. It began with a binder which cut the grain in the field, tied it in bundles, and left the bundles lying on the ground. Then the shockers carried the bundles into groups, carefully arranged so the air could dry the grain heads. Next, the pitchers forked the bundles from the shocks onto the rack wagons, which moved them to the threshing machines. The machines themselves were not so monstrous, but the power sources which operated them were the stuff from which myths arise: coal-fired, they belched black smoke, hissed steam, thumped and roared as the grain was separated and the chaff and straw were blown onto huge piles—the delight of farm kids as a playground. Finally the grain was collected in wagons and carted off for storage.

Threshing was a time for co-operation. Many of the machines were community-owned, for they were expensive and a threshing operation took at least a dozen men. It was a time to show off expertise, brawn—and pulling together.

But American ingenuity ended it. The combine came on the market, meaning less capital investment, far less labor, more independence. The steam engines shut down, the straw stacks disappeared, and farm wives no longer had to cook mountains of food for dozens of neighbors.

The farmers who owned the machine would do their own work first, and if there was any time left they'd do work for outsiders. The engineman would fire up at three or four in the morning, so steam would be up by six. We had to be up to make breakfast for the engineman after he got the fire going.

It took four head to pull the binder. If it was an eight-foot binder they usually had an extra two horses on lead, and a youngster driving them. I used to do that all day long.

If you got the bundles out of the row, the shocker would let you know about it, for it made his job just about impossible. He'd be running back and forth collecting bundles all day.

My mother always took supper for everyone out to the field so we wouldn't have to come in and lose time from shocking.

One of the best lickings I ever got from my dad was for walking on the straw pile. I didn't know that my feet left holes, and the holes filled with water when it rained, and the straw rotted.

The worst job was to sit back there all day and tie the wire on that stationary baler. It was plenty hot and dusty.

28

AUGUST 1933

"This month . . . we are putting before the 1,200,000 American farm families that grow wheat a proposal to reduce, perhaps as much as one fifth, their sowings of wheat for the next two years . . ."

HENRY A. WALLACE
Secretary of Agriculture

Combines like this one came in sometime around 1938. They were just so much cheaper. A six-foot combine that ran from a power take-off only cost about five hundred dollars, so individuals could afford them. That was the end of threshing, and the hard work and good times that went with it.

They had been cooking for threshers. Maybe up to twenty-five men would be at the table, or it would all have to be carried out to the field. It took a lot of doing.

CORN PICKING

A shucking peg fitted on your thumb. But this was a hook. We wore socks without feet over our arms. And mittens, but the mittens were always getting worn out.

IT WAS PROBABLY the toughest of harvest jobs. Unlike threshing, there just wasn't much glamour in walking a frost-covered corn row on a frigid morning, working up a sweat as you heaved ears, stripped from the wet stalk, into the wagon. It was field corn, of course, to feed the stock.

Ear corn, stored in ventilated cribs, gradually gave way to shelled corn, stripped from the cob by a Rube Goldbergian device that made almost as much noise as a threshing machine.

Like everything else in agriculture, it's a highly-mechanized operation now, as the corn heads, mounted on combines, poke their snouts down six or eight rows at a time, cutting the stalks, passing them through the innards of the combine, which find the ear, strip off the husk, pull the kernels loose, pump the kernels into a moving storage bin, and dump the rest, unwanted, back onto the field.

We'd get up at four and drive the horses three miles to shuck corn. Even if it was rain or icy we went ahead. I'd be out in the field long before the sun was up and hear those ears banging against the high side of the wagons. We tried to get through by Christmas, but shucking in the snow wasn't a bit unusual. Once I shucked a hundred and seventy-two bushels in a day, including scooping it into the bin. That was a real day's work and I've never forgotten the number.

It took all those belts and that great machine just to remove the kernels from the cobs—seemed like a lot of effort. But think how many trips to town we could save by carrying only the kernels, and leaving the useless cobs back on the farm.

That's the Missouri Pacific at Willis. The railroad came about 1898 and before World War I we were using the railroad to ship cattle and hogs to Saint Joe. We'd ship a whole carload and I'd ride the caboose. We used to drive the hogs on foot to the railroad—we had to do it early in the morning or in the evening, when it was cooler.

The railroad used to set the fields on fire with live coals from their engines. It was quite an experience to hear an automobile go by in the middle of the night honking its horn—that usually meant there was a grass fire going. The railroad section men would always be out fighting the fire if they caused it, and the railroad always settled up fair for the damage it caused.

In the drugstore was a little peephole they could look out through to see when the law was coming, because sometimes their alcohol wasn't used entirely for medicine.

DOWNTOWN

IT WAS LESS of a necessity, more of a luxury, than it is now. It was the post office, the blacksmith, the barber shop, and the general store. But forty years ago you could get along without these for a longer time than now. The car has made the distance to town seem shorter, and the trips have become more frequent, and the dependence on town greater.

But the small towns like Horton haven't necessarily benefited. Many have become ghost towns as roads improved to the point that it was easy to reach a larger town where more goods, or services, were available. The Middle West is pockmarked with deserted one-street towns. Willis, a tiny village where Wes took his country store pictures, is almost empty, although the store is still operating. Horton has lost population, and there are plenty of vacant stores, but it retains a semblance of being busy. Hiawatha, the county seat twelve miles away, is much more bustling than Horton or Willis.

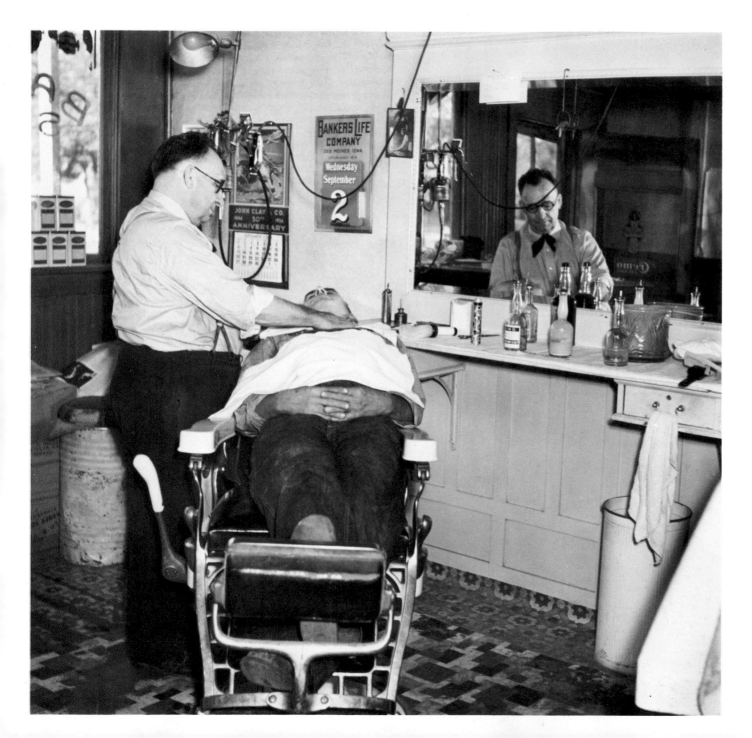

We used to get a twenty-five-cent haircut and a fifteen-cent shave—or thirty-five cents for both. Will Ross drove a horse and buggy to the barber shop from his farm twice a week without fail, but he was the only farmer around who went to all that trouble.

The blacksmith could do almost anything here. He made horseshoes from a straight piece of iron, not pre-formed shapes like they are now. But when motors came in he never learned to work with them, though he managed to stay in business until he died.

I went to work in the post office in 1934 and worked there thirty-five years. I was a widow with two little girls, and I thought I was fortunate to get the job because it was Depression time. When I started to work I got paid twenty-six dollars a month, full-time work. But my mother did laundry and practical nursing and we got along somehow. It wasn't easy sometimes, but we got the girls through high school.

The trough there at the base of the pump was for watering horses. All the teams that were working in the neighborhood would be brought in for water. The crossroads in front of the store, about where the photographer was standing, was the hot-rodder's corner. Even way back then we thought it was fun to spin dirt with a car's wheels, and the crossroads was big enough to make a complete turn in. Once I spun my *Model T* so fast it threw a tire off.

*In stores like Mathena's in those days farmers
pretty much traded out—they traded their cream,
eggs, and butter for their groceries and staples.
They don't do that much any more.*

49

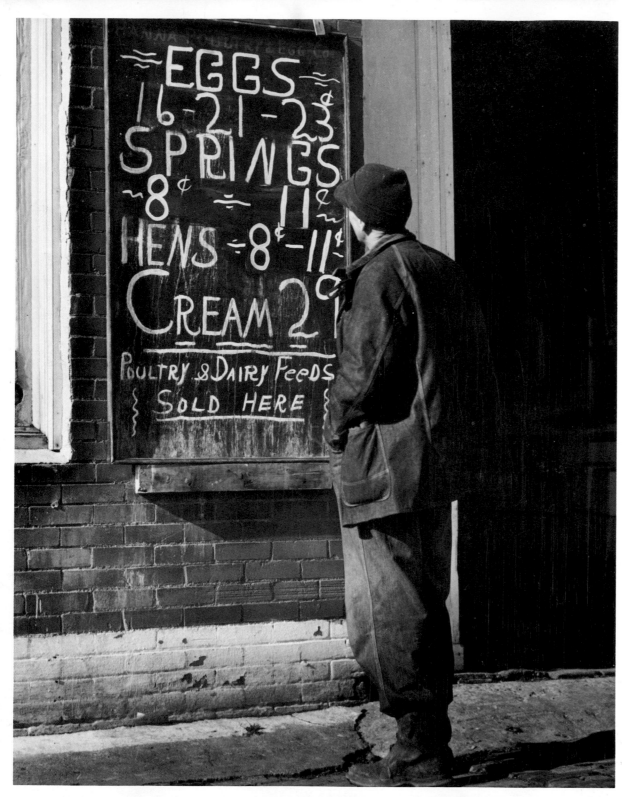

That's the price the farmer would get for the product he brought to the store. We sold hens for as little as nine cents a pound when we were first married.

My folks always drove into Horton on Saturday night after they got their first car—that was clear back in 1913. I remember my father was driving it and got headed for a ditch. Instead of putting his foot on the brake he kept shouting "Whoa!" and we ended up in the ditch with him still hollering "Whoa!"

"Between 1930 and 1933 one American farm in every four had been sold for debt or taxes."

HENRY A. WALLACE, *Secretary of Agriculture*

THE SALE

DURING the Depression it was likely to be a time of tension, for frequently a sale wasn't a voluntary liquidation. While auctions always have a certain excitement, it was often tempered then by the sadness of seeing a neighbor lose his possessions or the equity in his farm.

More than one sale ended, at least temporarily, when neighbors not only refused to bid on property, but forcibly saw to it that the bankers didn't bid either.

Once at George's farm sale the auctioneer said to him: "That's a good old engine we're selling, isn't it, George?" George just couldn't tell a lie. "Thing's not worth a damn," he said.

They used to say three moves from farm to farm was as bad as a fire.

That girl's exhibiting at the Horton fair, but we'd always go to the State fair at Topeka, take our purebred cattle, and stay the whole week.

THE FAIR

THERE WAS SOMETHING for everyone. And, in a day when television hadn't jaded the entertainment palate of the country, excitement built up headily the weeks before fair time.

Actually there were many fairs. Usually, the more local the fair, the less entertainment there was, and the more education and competition were provided.

But for most farm families in the Thirties there was a state fair, and here, although there was competition in animals and farm products, there were also innumerable distractions in the grandstand and along the professional midway. It was a time to explore, to visit, to imagine, and maybe to show off a little.

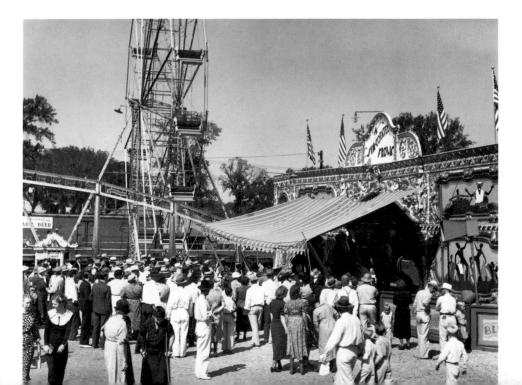

That thing? It's just a phone booth, but it was enough of a rarity so it was brought to the fair as an exhibit, and protected from the rain.

March 4, 1933

"More important, a host of unemployed citizens face the grim problem of existence, and an equally great number toil with little return. Only an optimist can deny the dark realities of the moment."

First Inaugural Address of Franklin Delano Roosevelt

POLITICS

POLITICS CAME to the farm in the Thirties with Franklin Roosevelt's New Deal. It has never left, and probably never will.

The erudite Henry Wallace, Secretary of Agriculture in President Roosevelt's Cabinet, brought with him the Biblical concept of establishing reserves from fat years to help out in lean times—but he failed to reckon with politicians and bureaucrats who could build storage facilities almost endlessly across the land, and promulgate regulations even faster.

Now, forty years later, we seem to have disposed of our surpluses for the first time since Wallace took office, and we are disposing of many of our restrictions on producing. And we're scared to death of the possible results.

> 1934
>
> "For a number of years I have been interested in the concept of the ever normal granary, a concept not greatly different from that of Joseph, in Bible days, or of the Confucians in ancient China."
>
> HENRY A. WALLACE, *Secretary of Agriculture*

We never had to register in those days. You just walked in and voted. Everyone knew everyone who showed up. If they didn't know you, you'd have to prove you lived in the district or get someone to vouch for you. But I don't think I was ever a judge of elections when anyone was contested: it was pretty rare.

I don't know why there were so many people in the bank when We. made his picture. I doubt it was taken during the bank rush in 1933

"Early in 1934 it became apparent that 1934 was to be a bad year; and as the spring came on, the drought attained a severity and extent beyond the memory of any living Americans."

HENRY A. WALLACE, *Secretary of Agriculture*

That's the REA crew putting up the electric in 1937 or 1938. Electrification is probably the thing which has changed agriculture and farm life more than any single thing.

CHORES

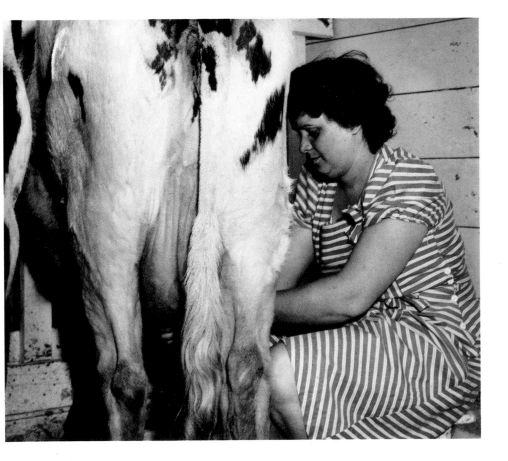

THEY SEEMED to go on endlessly. No one I ever knew who farmed in the Thirties was a late riser, and a forty-hour week for either husband or wife would have been laughable.

Two things have changed that. First, electricity and other power applications have reduced the physical labor that has to be put into chores.

And second, specialization has made many farmers' work seasonal. Dairy cows still have to be milked twice a day, every day, true. But I asked an Illinois county agent last year about livestock in the south end of his county. "Hell," he replied, "I don't think there's a farm animal bigger than a dog anywhere there. Those folks are cash-grain farmers, and they want to go to Florida in the winter."

The farm flock of chickens and the home-butchered hog are going the way of horse-drawn plows and hand milking.

I hated that separator with a purple passion. I was a city girl and when my mother-in-law told me I couldn't wash the separator with soap I didn't believe it was possible to get it clean any other way, so I went ahead and used soap. The whole insides got into a thick slime and it was a terrible mess. When we quit milking and doing our own separating, I used to wake up in the middle of the night and think "Oh, lands, I forgot to wash the separator." No matter how clean I kept it, that separator always made the kitchen smell milky. I was glad when we gave it up.

We had a slug of sheep down on that farm. Sheep were more important then. Lambs did well on lespedeza, and didn't take much grain. They'd clean up corn fields for you. But it takes a real top-notch man to handle them. We'd buy them in from Idaho in July or August and sell them out in January or February.

In those days hogs brought maybe four or five cents a pound, and the lard was in great demand. Today the price is ten times that, but no one wants lard.

LEISURE

BUT IF CHORES occupied endless time, there still seemed time for pleasure other than work.

It's hard to figure where that time came from. Partly, it came "off season." It wasn't by accident that fairs came at the end of a growing season, before the hustle of corn harvest. And so much leisure activity was homemade, or was in the village a few minutes away.

Then, too, there was no television—how many hours extra is that in everybody's day?

That bandstand was over west of Mathena's store. We not only had band concerts there, but sometimes we set up a big screen and showed movies too, right outdoors. Everyone in town came.

A fellow named Ludy used to play the harmonica, and when his wife would eavesdrop on the party line we could always hear Ludy's harmonica playing in the background.

First we tried it with a motorcycle engine, but it didn't have any power. This is a Model T that had been converted for airplane use. It worked, I'll tell you. It dragged us all over the ice. It was steered by the driver's feet, with a single runner in the back. It had a throttle, and a string that shut off the engine if we fell off. We made the propeller out of walnut—it was a common wood around here then—and we laminated it down at the railroad shops. Dangerous? The city should never have allowed it, we could have chopped up people something awful.

WINTER

THE IMPERFECTIONS of the farmscape were hidden by the anonymity of white, and the tempo slowed as the temperature dropped. Winter was a time of pleasure, and of recuperation, of gaining new strength for the exertions of spring.

The ice on the creek we skated on was always rough and rutty, but we didn't care. We'd build a campfire to keep warm, then go to someone's house to have oyster stew. I used to dream of skating and the ice was always smooth and perfect to start with, then all of a sudden I'd hit a rough place. I always thought then it must have been a reflection of the life I was leading.

They're harvesting ice here. The old ice refrigerators were pretty difficult way out in the country. We did have an ice delivery man, but by the time we got it into our refrigerators it was almost time to get more. Just the thought that a refrigerator could make ice was wonderful.

They still rope off a street in Horton for the kids to sled on. It's a busy street these days.

Most people'll probably think that's the mail man, but they're wrong. The mail man probably came through the road by truck. But one of the neighbors would pick up the mail from the boxes on horseback and deliver it right to everyone's house. That's the way we helped each other in those days.

83

I told the boys: "Remember, when Mom went to school we had to walk the whole way." One of them said: "What happened, Mom, did the bus break down?"

That was my favorite tree, and they destroyed it when they widened the road. I suppose that's progress.

WHATEVER HAPPENED
TO HORTON?

THE GLIB ANSWER is probably: not much.

The population of Horton has consistently decreased. The number of surrounding farmhouses that are vacant and tumbling down is greater today, though the acreage under cultivation probably hasn't lessened. It's just that fewer farmers can handle more acres.

Youngsters who have grown up on the farms and in the hamlets of Brown County, Kansas, are still moving toward the cities for their careers. There aren't many opportunities around Horton. No new industries have brought gigantic payrolls and real estate is hardly scarce.

Still, there are a few straws in the wind. The new apartments built on the main street are all rented, mostly by retired people who decided Horton was a good place to come back to. Living isn't expensive, everything is convenient, crime is almost non-existent, and people are friendly. Up at Willis a retired family just moved to town, back from California. There's no smog in Willis.

Even young families would like to come back. The tree-lined streets are safe for bicycles, the lake is fine for water-skiing, and the country club is looking for members. But it's hard to build a career here.

All in all, the place is remarkably the same as Wes showed it. People of course grow up, grow old, die. Agriculture has changed immensely. But Tag McManigal guided me to some of the places and people Wes had pictured, and I felt a continuity, a solidity, a peacefulness. Some people would say a stodginess, stagnation. Maybe. It depends on how you look at it.

Horton City Population
from the
Brown County Census

1925—4200
1930—4013
1935—3716
1940—2855
1945—2532
1950—2913
1955—2791
1960—2858
1965—2798
1970—2671

We built a new church there in 1954. We first moved the whole frame church to the west of where it stood . . . just hooked it up to a bulldozer and slid it clear off its foundations. Then we built a brand-new church on the original site, using the old church until we built the new one. Then we tore down the old church. We wanted to save the bell, but it was so heavy we didn't know how we could get it down from the tower. So we dozed a huge pile of soft earth, slid the bell to the outside of the tower, and dropped it into the mud. Nothing broke, and it's on a platform beside the new church now.

Why, that's Old Charlie. He was a bay, and his bad hock shows in the picture. He was harmless, safe for us kids. We still have the old buggy in the barn. You want to see it?

That's one thing's never changed around here. We still have the brightest skies anywhere. Smoke from factories is no problem: we've got no factories.

I'd like to be living back on a farm . . . my whole family'd prefer that.

95

A Technical Note

ABOUT WES McMANIGAL'S PHOTOGRAPHY

Hopefully, some of the readers of this book will be interested not only in farming in the 1930's, but also in photography.

Almost all of Wes's work was done on 4" x 5" negatives. The negatives have remained in remarkably good shape, though here and there some have faded. The film of the Thirties mostly had an ASA speed of 6 or 8, so you'll notice many of his pictures lack the depth of field we find common today—they had to be shot with the lens almost wide open.

His favorite camera was a 4 x 5 Speed Graphic. I've been unable to learn whether he had any lenses other than a standard focal length.

He also used that great workhorse of a camera, the 4 x 5 Graflex. For those of you not familiar with it, it was a huge single-lens reflex: big, heavy, and highly reliable. It was equipped with a cloth focal plane shutter which had a selection of four slits of varying widths, as well as a variable tension on the curtain, so that speeds from 1/30 to 1/1000 of a second could be used. The Graflex had a pouch which held twelve sheets of film. Once loaded, the twelve sheets could be rotated for exposure without further use of the darkroom.

Wes had an Ikonta B roll film camera, but of all his negatives I think there are fewer than a hundred which are less than 4 x 5, so he apparently disdained the smaller sizes. 35mm cameras were available in his day, but they weren't widely used.

In the darkroom, Wes relied on a Solar enlarger. It had a large metal light reflector, and the projection light went through several diffusion glasses, rather than through condensers.

Although Wes took a good many flash pictures, flash equipment was cumbersome, and complex. Shutters did not have built-in synchronization, but relied on battery-operated solenoids which mechanically pulled the shutter release, also firing the flashbulb. Electronic flash was, of course, unknown.

Because shutter speeds frequently had to be so slow, they wouldn't stop ordinary motion. Wes often had to warn his people to "hold it!" Thus a good many of his pictures aren't truly candid, and some seem somewhat stiff and artificial.

And if his subjects seem partial to Levi overalls, this wasn't exactly chance. Wes took many of the pictures Levi used in its advertising and he dressed his friends from a big carton of new overalls Levi sent to Horton each year.